Celebrating Constitution Day

Grades K–3

Authors

Roben Alarcon, M.A.Ed

Christi E. Parker, M.A.Ed

Garth Sundem, M.M.

Shell Educational Publishing

Editor
Gillian Eve Makepeace

Project Manager
Corinne Burton, M.A.Ed.

Editor-in-Chief
Sharon Coan, M.S.Ed.

Creative Director
Lee Aucoin

Imaging
Deb Brown

Production Manager
Phil Garcia

Illustration Manager
Timothy J. Bradley

Cover Design
Neri Garcia

Illustrator
Ana Clark

Cover Art
The National Archives

Standards
Compendium, Copyright 2004 McREL

Publisher
Rachelle Cracchiolo, M.S.Ed.

Shell Educational Publishing
5301 Oceanus Drive
Huntington Beach, CA 92649-1030
www.tcmpub.com
ISBN-0-7439-0259-9
©2005 Shell Educational Publishing
Reprinted, 2006
Made in U.S.A.

Table of Contents

The History Behind Our Constitution

The United States Constitution was not America's first written system of government. The Articles of Confederation, ratified in 1781, holds that honor. It was a flawed system from the start, however, and quickly showed signs of detrimental problems. Government leaders realized that the wording would have to change for the system to succeed.

America's leaders came together to make a few revisions, but soon realized that the entire document would have to be modified. In fact it was changed so much that they gave it a new name, the Constitution. It gave more power to the central government, and detailed the three branches we have today—legislative, executive, and judicial. Not everyone was pleased with the final outcome, and there was some doubt that it would be ratified. A group of men decided to get together and encourage ratification through anonymous letters written to newspapers. Under the pen name *Publius*, John Jay, Alexander Hamilton, and James Madison wrote essays explaining the Constitution and encouraging the states to accept it. Those letters later became known as *The Federalist Papers*. Whether these letters had much of an influence is debatable. Regardless, in 1788 the document was ratified by two-thirds of the states and our new government was under way.

Constitution Basics

The United States Constitution essentially explains the specific responsibilities of the three branches of government. The legislative branch creates the laws, while the executive branch enforces them. It is the duty of the judicial branch to interpret the law through the court system. Even though the three branches increase the strength of the central government, a system of checks and balances was put in place as a way to avert an abuse of power. For example, the president has the task of nominating Supreme Court judges, but then the Senate must vote to confirm each nomination. This is one way that the legislative branch "checks" on the executive branch. This separation of power holds each branch accountable and helps to ensure overall integrity. In addition to these details, the Constitution includes an explanation of the role of the states and how our country works together as a whole.

Adding a Bill of Rights

Right away a major concern with the new document was it lacked individual rights. The colonists simply could not forget the tyranny of England and were terrified of losing their civil liberties once again. Even though James Madison originally thought a list of personal rights wasn't necessary, he changed his mind and worked with Congress to come up with twelve amendments to the new Constitution. Ten were ratified by the states and those amendments officially became the Bill of Rights. Only seventeen more amendments have been made over the course of the last 200 years.

The system developed by our founding fathers is an amazing document that has remained effective for hundreds of years, proving its relevance time and again. The United States Constitution is clearly a great source of pride for our country.

What is Constitution Day?

The final draft of the United States Constitution was signed in Philadelphia, Pennsylvania, on September 17, 1787. Months later, enough states had ratified it (nine out of thirteen) to officially make it our nation's new system of government.

In the years following, many citizens of the United States have celebrated the creation of the Constitution at various times during the month of September. One particular group, the Daughters of the American Revolution (DAR), has been especially vocal in its desire to preserve the history of our Constitution and convey its true meaning to all Americans. In fact, the DAR even erected the only structure dedicated to the Constitution—Constitution Hall. This memorial is registered as a national historic landmark.

In 1955, the DAR began actively petitioning Congress to proclaim the week following September 17 as Constitution Week, in observance of our treasured document. Because of the group's effort and dedication, Senator William F. Knowland of California formally initiated a Senate Joint Resolution to make Constitution Week an annual event and on August 2, 1956, President Eisenhower signed the motion into public law. Constitution Week was now official.

Fifty years later, in 2005, the Constitution was in the news once again. President George W. Bush signed public law 108-447 requiring all educational institutions that receive federal funds to teach the United States Constitution on September 17 (or the closest school day if it falls on a weekend). In addition, the law states that educators must be provided with the necessary teaching materials in order to fulfill the mandate. Designating September 17 as Constitution Day demonstrates the value that our government places on this historical document. Students around the nation will now have multiple opportunities to grasp its significance.

Constitution Day in the Classroom

Celebrating Constitution Day was written in an effort to supply educators in the primary grades with lessons that will effectively make the Constitution meaningful to their students. Each lesson focuses on a significant aspect of the Constitution so that the crucial elements of our government system are conveyed. In addition, national symbols and patriotism are expressed in ways that help even the youngest of students get a sense of our country and what being an American means.

The activities in this book strive to simplify this complicated subject and bring it to life for the students, allowing them to grasp the Constitution as a whole. Though arranged by grade level, the lessons were designed to work across the primary grades with simple modifications. Since all portions of the book relate to the Constitution, it would be reasonable to choose those lessons that you feel are appropriate for your class. Furthermore, each lesson has activities that address the various levels of Bloom's Taxonomy of the Cognitive Domain. Beginning with basic comprehension and progressively moving up to extensive understanding, Bloom's

Constitution Day in the Classroom (cont.)

Taxonomy is widely used as a guide to measuring learning. This book uses these levels to promote higher order thinking for those that have successfully attained the lower level skills. Use your own discretion in deciding which levels are most suitable for your students.

Now that schools are mandated to teach the Constitution annually at all grade levels, students will be receiving instruction on this topic repeatedly. Over time, they should establish a rich background knowledge of our system of government, one they can build upon year after year. We hope *Celebrating Constitution Day* will assist your students in this endeavor.

National Symbols
Kindergarten Lesson Plans

Objective

Understands how democratic values came to be, and how they have been exemplified by people, events, and symbols, such as knowing the history of American symbols.
McREL K-4 History Standard 4, Level 1.8.

Materials

★ copies of *Fly Like An Eagle* (page 10)

★ copies of *Design a Flag* (page 11)

★ copies of *Symbol Sort* (page 12)

★ art supplies and blank paper

★ *Uncle Sam and Old Glory* by Delano West and Jean C. West (optional)

★ Pictures of a United States flag, a bald eagle, and a model of the Statue of Liberty

Procedure

1. Ask the students to brainstorm items that remind them of the United States and their freedom. (You might first want to discuss the meaning of freedom.) Write their suggestions on the board. Explain to the students that the bald eagle, the flag, and the other items mentioned are all symbols of the United States and show what our country is about.

2. Next, show students items that include a bald eagle, the United States flag, and the Statue of Liberty. Ask them what comes to mind when they see these items.

3. Share some of the information from *Background Information* (page 9) with your students. You will need to be selective for your younger students. Go over the bolded words before reading. You might choose to copy the information for the students so that they can follow along.

4. After you have discussed *Background Information* with the students, put them in pairs. Give each pair *Fly Like An Eagle* (page 10). Discuss the directions with the students. Then, give them the opportunity to complete the graphic organizer concerning what they learned as they read the background information. Encourage students to write down or draw at least one thing they have learned about each of the symbols of the United States. You may also choose to do this activity as a class.

5. After students have completed their organizers, give them a copy of *Design a Flag* (page 11). This image can be found on the Library of Congress website at this URL address: http://hdl.loc.gov/loc.pnp/cph.3g02791. As a class, answer the *Design a Flag Questions* (page 8) about the picture of Betsy Ross and the flag. Then, ask students to complete the activity underneath the primary source picture.

6. To assess your students' learning, go over each activity in the *Bloom's Taxonomy Chart* (page 8) with the class. Assign each student an activity or allow them to choose their own. All of these activities are based on Bloom's Taxonomy of Cognitive Development.

7. Finally, for an extension, refer to *Extension Activity* (page 8).

Design a Flag Questions

★ What do you see in the picture?

★ Does the flag look the same as it does today?

★ Who do you think is holding the flag?

★ Do you think the people in the picture like the flag?

★ Who do you think the man is standing near the flag?

Bloom's Taxonomy Chart

Knowledge: List three United States symbols. Then, draw a picture of each.

Comprehension: What is your favorite United State's symbol? Explain why you like it.

Application: What is your school's symbol? Find out, and draw a picture of it.

Analysis: Find a picture of your state flag. Name or draw two ways it is like the United States flag. Name or draw two ways it is not like the United States flag. You can use a Venn diagram to compare the flags if you would like.

Synthesis: A symbol is a picture or item that tells about something. What symbol would tell about you? Draw a picture of a symbol that would describe you.

Evaluation: Benjamin Franklin wanted the wild turkey to be the national symbol, but Thomas Jefferson and John Adams did not like it. Do you think the turkey would make a good national symbol? Why or why not?

Extension Activity

Use the book *Uncle Sam and Old Glory* by Delano West and Jean C. West to complete *Symbol Sort* (page 12).

❶ Read the book *Uncle Sam and Old Glory* aloud to students. You do not need to read the entire book. You might choose just the symbols mentioned in the lesson plus a couple of the symbols that would be of most interest to the students.

❷ Next, divide the class in half. Name one half "Freedom" and the other "Liberty."

❸ Make a list, or draw, the following symbols on the board or overhead: Uncle Sam, United States flag, Liberty Bell, bald eagle, "Yankee Doodle," and the Statue of Liberty. Tell students to refer to this list as they play the game.

❹ Read a clue from *Symbol Sort*. Give only one clue at a time. The team that figures out the clue first gets the points. If they guess the symbol on the first clue, award three points. On the second clue, award two points, and on the third clue, award one point.

Background Information

The Constitution is the **document**, or paper, that explains the rules and laws in America. It also tells other countries that we want to be free from rule. America has a lot of symbols that show other countries what the Constitution means to Americans. Three of those symbols are the United States flag, the bald eagle, and the Statue of Liberty.

The United States Flag

On June 14th, America celebrates Flag Day. That is because our first flag was approved by the **Continental Congress** on June 14, 1777. Many people believe that Betsy Ross made the first flag. This first flag had 13 stripes and 13 stars. The stars were on a blue background. But, in 1818 more states became a part of our country. So, the flag was changed to make the stars always equal to the number of states. The 13 stripes stand for the 13 **colonies**, or the first states. The Continental Congress never said why they chose red, white, and blue for the colors. People believe that blue means **justice**, red stands for strength, and the white represents purity. Sometimes, the flag is called "Old Glory" or the "Stars and Stripes."

The Bald Eagle

The bald eagle was chosen to be the national **emblem**, or symbol, in 1782. It was the idea of a man called William Burton, because he thought the bald eagle was strong and powerful.

In 1776, Benjamin Franklin, Thomas Jefferson, and John Adams were first asked to decide what the national symbol should be. These men helped write the Constitution, but, they could not agree on a symbol. Benjamin Franklin wanted it to be a wild turkey. Adams and Jefferson said no to that idea. In the end, the bald eagle was chosen.

The bald eagle is only found in the United States and most of them live in Alaska. You can see images of them on a lot of buildings in the United States. There are also pictures of them on United States money.

The Statue of Liberty

The Statue of Liberty is a symbol of **freedom**. It was a gift to the United States from France. France is a country on the **continent** of Europe. The same man who built the Eiffel Tower in Paris created the iron frame of the statue. But, a Frenchman named Frederic-Auguste designed the actual statue. You have to travel to New York City to visit the Statue of Liberty. It has been there since 1886.

The entire name of the statue is "Liberty Enlightening the World." Chains are around the feet of the statue. The right hand of the statue holds a torch. It stands for **liberty**. The left hand of Lady Liberty holds a book called a tablet. It has the date July 4, 1776 written on it. That is the day the United States said they wanted to be free from Britain–the country that once controlled the United States. There are seven spikes on the Statue of Liberty's crown. They stand for the seven seas and the seven continents.

Name: _____

Date: _____

Directions: Fill this bald eagle with words or pictures to show what you have learned about the flag, the bald eagle, and the Statue of Liberty.

What I learned about the Statue of Liberty

What I learned about the bald eagle

What I learned about the United States flag

Name: _____

Date: _____

The painting below is Betsy Ross and two small girls showing the United States flag to George Washington and three other men.

Courtesy of The Library of Congress

Directions: Pretend that you are Betsy Ross. George Washington has asked you to create a flag for the United States of America. Use crayons, paints, or other art supplies to create your own original flag for the United States.

Symbol Sort
Student Reproducible

Name: _____

Date: _____

Symbol 1
1. Ding Dong!
2. This symbol cracks me up!
3. I live in Philadelphia.

I am _____.

Symbol 2
1. I was sung to make fun of the soldiers that were fighting for America's freedom.
2. I was also sung by the men who fought for our freedom as they marched into battle.
3. I talk about macaroni, but it isn't the kind with cheese.

I am _____.

Symbol 3
1. Many say I was started by a butcher named Sam Wilson.
2. I am a cartoon that is on posters saying, "I Want You!"
3. I have a beard, and I like to wear a blue coat and red and white pants so I look like the United States flag.

I am _____.

Symbol 4
1. I am sometimes called "Old Glory" or the "Stars and Stripes."
2. A lot of people say that Betsy Ross was the first to sew me up.
3. My favorite colors are red, white, and blue.

I am _____.

Symbol 5
1. I am the United States' symbol of strength.
2. Ben Franklin liked turkeys better than me.
3. I was almost extinct because of hunters.

I am _____.

Symbol 6
1. I live in New York City.
2. I was a gift from France.
3. My nickname is "Lady Liberty."

I am _____.

Being a Classroom Citizen
Kindergarten Lesson Plans

Objective

Understands how democratic values came to be, and how they have been exemplified by people, events, and symbols by understanding ways in which such fundamental values as fairness, protection of individual rights, and responsibility for the common good have been applied by different groups of people (e.g., students and personnel in the local school.)
McREL K-4 History Standard 4, Level 1.3

Materials

★ copy of *A Classroom Citizen to All* (page 15)

★ copies of *Being a Citizen Means . . .* (page 16)

★ copies of *Voting* (page 17)

★ copies of *Good Citizen, Bad Citizen* (page 18)

★ art supplies and blank paper

★ craft sticks

Procedure

1. Have students sit in a circle around the room. As you go around the circle, ask each student to complete this sentence: "I help in our classroom by . . ."

2. After each student has completed that sentence, go around the circle and complete the next sentence: "In our classroom, I get to . . ."

3. Once the students have completed their sentences aloud, write a couple on the board and have them complete their two sentences on sheets of paper. Next, have them draw a picture of them doing the things in the sentence, or take a picture of them doing those things. Combine all of the students' pages to create a Classroom Citizens Class Book.

4. Tell the students that they are all citizens of the classroom. Write the word "citizen" on the board. Explain to them that the United States Constitution says that anyone born in the United States is a citizen. So, because students are part of your classroom, they too are citizens of your class.

5. Read the poem at the top of *A Classroom Citizen to All* (page 15) aloud to the students. The poem is about the duties of a classroom citizen compared to a United States citizen. Give each student *Being a Citizen Means . . .* (page 16). Have them complete the graphic organizer as a class, or allow them to work individually and then discuss them as a class.

6. You might also choose to discuss with students what the poem said about being a United States citizen and list other rights and responsibilities that were not mentioned in the poem.

7. After students have completed their organizers, show them *Voting* (page 17). This image can be found on the Library of Congress website at this URL address: http://hdl.loc.gov/loc.pnp/cph.3b22537. Complete *Voting Activity and Questions* (page 14).

8. To assess your students' learning, go over each activity in the *Bloom's Taxonomy Chart* (page 14) with the class. Assign each student an activity or allow them to choose their own. All of these activities are based on Bloom's Taxonomy of Cognitive Development.

9. Finally, for an extension, refer to the *Extension Activity* (page 14).

Being a Classroom Citizen
Kindergarten Lesson Plans (cont.)

Voting Activity and Questions

1 Tell students that this photograph shows women voting for the first time. Explain that voting is when we get to show what we think about choices. Explain that although women are citizens of the United States, they have not always had the right to vote.

2 Ask students to look at the photograph. Ask the following questions.

★ How do the women seem to be feeling?

★ Why is voting important?

★ What does voting let you do?

3 Next, hold a mock election in your class. Allow students to vote on anything from rewards, to a class president, to what snack to eat.

4 After voting, ask the students if they felt the same way as the people in the picture. Explain to them that voting is a right written in the Constitution for citizens of the United States and allows you to take part in making decisions.

Bloom's Taxonomy Chart

Knowledge: Think of two rights you have as a classroom citizen. Tell them to your classroom neighbor sitting next to you.

Comprehension: Draw a picture of responsibilities you have as a classroom citizen.

Application: What are some things you can do to be a good citizen at home? Draw a picture to explain.

Analysis: Do you have the right to vote in your classroom? Do you like voting? Does it help the class make decisions? Answer these questions for your teacher.

Synthesis: If you were the teacher, what responsibilities would you ask your students to have as classroom citizens? Cut out pictures from a magazine, and glue them on a piece of blank paper to show these responsibilities.

Evaluation: To become a United States citizen, you must either be born in the United States, or you must take a test. Is this a fair way to become a citizen? Tell your teacher your opinion.

Extension Activity

Use the poem from the lesson to complete this extension activity.

1 The poem outlines several things a citizen of the United States should do. Have students cut out the faces on *Good Citizen, Bad Citizen* (page 18). Have them color and glue them on craft sticks.

2 Below the poem on page 15 are several situations. Cut the situations into strips. Allow students to take turns choosing a strip from a jar. Read the strip aloud and have students hold up the correct face depending on the situation.

3 Discuss with the students how each of the children in the stories could be good citizens.

Name: _____

Date: _____

A Classroom Citizen to All

A United State's citizen is someone who,

Has rights and freedoms just like you.

A United State's citizen is protected,

And they get to say who should be elected.

But, a United States citizen has things he must do,

Like respect the law and pay taxes, too.

So, being a citizen in your classroom will mean,

You have duties and rights that should always be seen.

Follow the rules, help others, and listen,

Indeed, it will make you a good classroom citizen.

Paula sees crayons on the floor of her classroom. She didn't spill them, so she decides not to pick them up. Is she being a good or bad citizen?

Thomas sees a classmate fall down at recess. He quickly runs to her to see if she needs help. Is he being a good or bad citizen?

The teacher holds up Sara's painting for the class to see. Joey yells out that he doesn't like the painting. Is he being a good or bad citizen?

The teacher tells all of the students the rules on the first day of class. Katie says she doesn't have to follow the rules. Is she being a good or bad citizen?

The teacher tells the class that they are going to vote on their afternoon snack. Sam says he doesn't have to vote because he doesn't like making choices. Is he being a good or bad citizen?

Bryce needs help picking up the blocks. So, Emily stops to help him. Is she being a good or bad citizen?

Being a Citizen Means . . .
Student Reproducible

Name: _____

Date: _____

What makes a good citizen? What are things you should do as a citizen in your classroom? What are some things you get to do because you are a classroom citizen?

Directions: Draw pictures of things you get to do in your classroom because you are a citizen of your classroom. Draw pictures of things you should do in your classroom because you are a classroom citizen.

As a classroom citizen, I get to . . .

As a classroom citizen, I must . . .

Name: _____

Date: _____

Courtesy of The Library of Congress

Good Citizen

Bad Citizen

Democracy in the Classroom
Grade One Lesson Plans

Objective

Understands how democratic values came to be, and how they have been exemplified by people, events, and symbols by understanding ways in which such fundamental values as fairness, protection of individual rights, and responsibility for the common good have been applied by different groups of people (e.g., students and personnel in the local school.)
McREL K-4 History Standard 4, Level 1.3

Materials

★ copies of *Leader of the Class Reader's Theater* (pages 22–23)

★ copies of *Creating a Classroom Democracy* (page 24)

★ copies of *If I Were Class President* (page 25)

★ art supplies and blank paper

★ old magazines

Procedure

1. Create a poster that says "Do You Want to Be President?" Display the poster where students can see it as they come into the classroom.

2. Tell students that a special event is coming to the classroom. They will be voting for a class leader.

3. Write the word "democracy" on the board. Explain to students that the Constitution was written so that our government would be a democracy. This means that the government is run by the people of the country, and those people have choices.

4. Tell the students that the classroom is also a democracy in some ways. Ask the class what choices the have in the classroom. They might give ideas such as choosing which snack to eat, how to play at recess, or what art supplies to use to create a project.

5. Next, tell them that in a democracy the people get to vote for their leaders. The person with the most votes wins. Explain to the students that they are going to choose a classroom leader. This leader will be in charge of special tasks in the classroom. (You can designate what jobs the leader will have, such as handing out lunch tickets, or passing out papers.)

6. To show students how a democracy in the classroom will work, do *Leader of the Class Reader's Theater* (pages 22–23) as a class. The script will introduce your students to the concept of democracy and how it applies to the classroom. Since reader's theater concentrates on fluency and the understanding of the text, it is not necessary for there to be props or costumes. You may simply wish to seat the performing students on stools in front of the room.

   If you do not feel your students can read the skit fluently, you may also record the script as students follow along, using different voices for each character. Or, you may ask the higher level students to read the script.

   Even though there are only six parts, allow the other members of the class to follow along as they read. Explain that the script can be read a couple more times so that everyone has a turn reading. The repeated readings will also help students with their fluency.

Procedure *(cont.)*

7 Before reading the script, you might choose to go over the following words with the students: elected, England, freedoms, government, president, vote.

8 After you have performed the reader's theater, pass out *Creating a Classroom Democracy* (page 24). Explain to students that they too are going to be running for classroom leader. As a classroom leader, they must decide what choices other classmates should get to vote on in the class. Ask them to fill out the graphic organizer with ways to have a democracy in the classroom.

9 After students have completed the graphic organizer, go over the choices they feel they should have in their classroom. Ask them if their choices are for the good of all of their classmates. For example, if they write they should get to vote on having recess all day, ask them if this would be good for them. What would they miss out on?

10 After students have completed their organizers, show them *If I Were Class President* (page 25). This image can be found on the Library of Congress website at this URL address: http://hdl.loc.gov/loc.pnp/cph.3c17116. As a class, complete *If I Were Class President Questions and Activity* below.

11 After students have completed the primary source activity, allow them to raise their hands if they would like to run for class leader. Write their names on the board. Then, allow students to secretly vote for class leader. Explain to them that they should vote for the person that will do the best job.

12 To assess your students' learning, go over each activity in the *Bloom's Taxonomy Chart* (page 21) with the class. Assign each student an activity or allow them to choose their own. All of these activities are based on Bloom's Taxonomy of Cognitive Development.

13 Finally, for an extension, refer to the *Extension Activity* (page 21).

If I Were Class President Questions and Activity

1 Ask students the following questions.

★ Who is the man in the picture?

★ What do you know about George Washington?

2 Explain to students that George Washington was the first person to be elected president of the United States. He won the most votes and that is how he became president. Tell students that in a democracy the president makes the choices for the people after he is elected.

3 Ask students to help you create a list of things they would do in the classroom if they were voted class leader. What would they do to change their classroom? How would they help their classmates?

4 Have each student complete the sentence on *If I Were Class President* (page 25). Ask the students that want to run for president of the class to share their ideas. Explain that the rest of the class should listen, so that they can vote for the person that would help the class the most.

Bloom's Taxonomy Chart

Knowledge: Draw a picture of two things you get to do in a democracy.

Comprehension: What is a democracy? Write the definition in your own words.

Application: Do you have a democracy at home? Are there any choices you get to make? Write down two things you get to choose to do, or vote on, at home. Draw a picture of two things you would like to get to vote on at home, but you don't.

Analysis: Is it better to have choices? Name one reason why having choices is good. Name one reason why having choices can be bad.

Synthesis: Pretend that you have been asked to create a government for your country. Would you create a democracy where people can choose, or would you rule the government and make all of the decisions? Make a poster of how your government would work, and what you would let the people do.

Evaluation: Complete this sentence: A classroom democracy is good because . . .

Extension Activity

1 Hang a large poster on one side of the room that says "Democracy." Hang another poster on the other side of the room that says "Not a Democracy."

2 Explain to students that you are going to read them various statements. If the sentence you read shows something that happens in a democracy, have them stand next to the "Democracy" sign. If it shows something that is not a democracy, have them stand near the "Not a Democracy Sign."

★ Your teacher tells you to raise your hand if you want to go to the children's museum for your field trip.

★ Your mother asks you and your sisters to vote on what to eat for dinner.

★ Your mother says "We are having green beans for dinner, and that is final!"

★ The teacher tells you that you must complete all of your math problems. You don't have a vote in the matter.

★ The teacher asks you to vote on a class pet.

★ The principal asks you to choose the teacher of the year.

3 Discuss with the students if they like living in a democracy. Why or why not?

Characters
Constitution Man
Mrs. Voter (classroom teacher)
Stanley, Frank, Sally, Sue (four students in Mrs. Voter's class)

Mrs. Voter has just told her students they will be voting for a class leader when a surprise guest shows up, the United States Constitution.

Mrs. Voter: Okay class, who can tell me what a democracy is?

Stanley: Oh, no! I always forget these big words! Democracy? Democracy? What is it?

Sally: Oh, Mrs. Voter, I know! Pick me, pick me!

Mrs. Voter: Okay, Sally, what is a democracy?

Sally: It's when the people make the choices in their country. They get to vote on their leaders.

Mrs. Voter: That is very good, Sally. The United States is a democracy. That means we vote for our president and other leaders. But, we have a democracy in our classroom too.

Frank: We do? How?

Sue: Do we have a democracy because we get to vote on what to do for Fun Fridays?

Stanley: Or because we get to choose what centers to go to?

Mrs. Voter: That's right, and today we are going to choose a president for the day. So, we will get to vote on who will be our class leader. They will have special jobs, like passing out snacks and leading us in the pledge. But, before we begin our election, does anyone know what paper has the United States' rules for democracy written on it?

Frank: Hmmm? What could it be?

In walks a small, rolled paper with eyes. The students are amazed, but eager to find out who he is.

Constitution Man: Mrs. Voter, if you don't mind, I would love to tell the students about a democracy. After all, I am the paper that lists how the United States' democracy will work.

Sue: Who are you?

Constitution Man: I am the United States Constitution, and I am more than 200 years old. The leaders of our country did not want to be ruled by a king or queen. So, they made sure the people would have choices.

Sally: That's right. They had just become free from the king of England. They didn't want to be ruled again like that.

Constitution Man: So, they wrote me. And I have laws that everyone in the United States must follow. But, I have a list of rights, too. And one of those rights is getting to vote for our leaders. The leader with the most votes wins. That is what happens in a democracy.

Stanley: Democracy. What a wonderful idea! So, who gets to run for our classroom leader?

Mrs. Voter: In a democracy, almost anyone can run.

Sue: Oh, can I?

Frank: And me too?

Sally: I don't think I want to run, but I definitely want to vote!

Stanley: Oh, to be president for a day! I want to run!

Mrs. Voter: Well, Constitution Man, it looks like you have really gotten my students excited about living in a democracy.

Constitution Man: Well then, my job here is done! Enjoy running for classroom leader!

Name: _____

Date: _____

What choices do you think you should have in your classroom? What things should your classmates get to vote on?

Directions: Cut out pictures from magazines or draw pictures of things you should get to vote on in your classroom. Put the pictures on the Constitution below. Make sure the ideas will help your classmates. For example, it wouldn't be a good idea to vote for no homework because homework helps you learn.

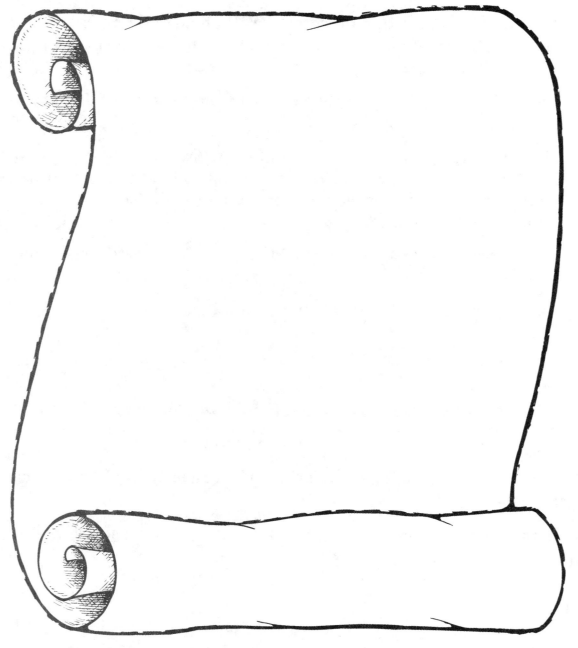

Name:_____

Date:_____

Courtesy of The Library of Congress

Directions: Complete the following sentence.

If I were class president, I would . . .

_____

_____

What Does the Pledge Mean, Anyway?

Grade One Lesson Plans

Objective

Understands how democratic values came to be, and how they have been exemplified by people, events, and symbols by knowing the Pledge of Allegiance and patriotic songs, poems, and sayings that were written long ago, and understands their significance. McREL K-4 History Standard 4, Level II-10

Materials

★ *I Pledge Allegiance*, by Bill Martin and Michael Sampson

★ copies of *The Meaning of the Pledge of Allegiance* (page 28)

★ copies of *What the Pledge Means to Me* (page 29)

★ copies of *Recite After Me* (page 30)

★ copies of *Pledge Scramble Cards* (page 31)

★ art supplies and blank paper

Procedure

1 Bring the United States flag into the classroom. Ask students if they know the Pledge of Allegiance. You may also choose to say the pledge at this time. Ask the students if they know the meaning of the words in the Pledge of Allegiance. Allow them to make guesses for what the words mean.

2 Write the word "allegiance" on the board. Explain to them that an allegiance is a promise to be true and loyal to something. So, when you say the Pledge of Allegiance, you are promising to be true to the United States.

3 Read students the book *I Pledge Allegiance*, by Bill Martin and Michael Sampson. If this book is not available to you, share *The Meaning of the Pledge of Allegiance* (page 28) with the students. As you read the book with the students, discuss the meaning of the words in the Pledge.

4 After students have learned about the meaning of the words in the Pledge of Allegiance, allow them to complete *What the Pledge Means to Me* (page 29). You may choose for them to complete the organizer in groups, individually, or as a class.

5 After students have completed their organizers, show *Recite After Me* (page 30) of students saying the Pledge of Allegiance. This image can be found on the Library of Congress website at this URL address: http://hdl.loc.gov/loc.pnp/cph.3a16954. As a class, complete *Recite After Me Questions and Activity* (page 27).

6 To assess your students' learning, go over each activity in the *Bloom's Taxonomy Chart* (page 27) with the class. Assign each student an activity or allow them to choose their own. All of these activities are based on Bloom's Taxonomy of Cognitive Development.

7 Finally, for an extension, refer to *Extension Activity* (page 27).

What Does the Pledge Mean, Anyway?
Grade One Lesson Plans (cont.)

Recite After Me Questions and Activity

1 Ask students the following questions.
- ★ What are the children doing?
- ★ Do they appear to take the pledge seriously, or are they being silly?
- ★ Why should you be serious when you say the pledge?
- ★ What is different in the picture from when you say the pledge?

2 Explain to the students that when the pledge is being said, they should stand with their right hand over their heart. But, it was not always this way. Up until 1942, the pledge was said with the right arm pointing out. This was changed during World War II.

Bloom's Taxonomy Chart

Knowledge: Choose one sentence from the Pledge of Allegiance. Draw a picture of its meaning.

Comprehension: Choose one sentence from the Pledge of Allegiance. In your own words, tell your neighbor what it means.

Application: With a partner, rewrite the Pledge of Allegiance making it easier to understand for young children.

Analysis: The following is the Boy Scout Oath, or pledge. What do you think the words to this pledge mean? Does it have any of the same words found in the Pledge of Allegiance? Work with a partner to answer these questions.

> On my honor I will do my best,
> To do my duty to God and my country and to obey the Scout Law;
> To help other people at all times;
> To keep myself physically strong, mentally awake, and morally straight.

Synthesis: A pledge is simply a promise to be true to something. Pledges do not just have to be to your country. You can also say a pledge to your church, a special group, your school, or even your parents.

Bloom's Taxonomy Chart (cont.)

Create your own pledge. Who would you say the pledge to? Your pledge can be just one sentence or an entire paragraph.

Evaluation: Complete this sentence: The best part of the Pledge of Allegiance is . . . because . . . .

Extension Activity

1 To be sure the students have comprehended the words to the pledge, play the following pledge scrabble game.

2 Divide the class into small groups. Give each group the *Pledge Scramble Cards* (page 31). Have them cut out the cards and mix them up.

3 Then, show them a picture from the book *I Pledge Allegiance*, or read a section of the pledge. Tell students to find the words that belong to that picture. Have them hold them up when their group finds them.

4 You may choose to give points for the group that finds the correct words first. You may also choose to deduct points to make sure the groups are not just holding up cards at random.

Name: _____

Date: _____

The Pledge of Allegiance was first made public on September 8, 1892. It was written in a Boston magazine. The author was Francis Bellamy. Even though the pledge has changed a little over the years, it is still said to show loyalty to the flag and to the United States. The Pledge of Allegiance is a saying that tells others how the people of the United States feel about our freedom, which is written about in the Constitution.

These are the words to the Pledge of Allegiance, and what they mean:

I pledge allegiance to the flag of the United States of America—I promise to be loyal and true to the United States and the flag that is a symbol for it.

and to the Republic for which it stands,—The United States is a Republic. That means we have leaders that are chosen by the people. I promise to be loyal to the leaders too.

one Nation under God, indivisible,—The United States is one nation. It can not be torn apart or divided. It will always stand as one.

with liberty and justice for all.—Every person in the United States should be treated fairly. They are all free to make choices, too.

What the Pledge Means to Me

Student Reproducible

Name: _____

Date: _____

Now that you have learned the meaning of the words to the Pledge of Allegiance, what do they mean to you? The words to the Pledge of Allegiance are written below on the flag.

Directions: Create a picture on the stripes to show the meaning of those words.

I pledge allegiance to the flag of the United States of America

and to the Republic for which it stands . . . .

one Nation, under God, indivisible . . . .

with liberty and justice for all.

Name: _____

Date: _____

Courtesy of The Library of Congress

Directions: In your group, create a list of rules for saying the Pledge of Allegiance. How should it be said? How should one act when saying it? Draw pictures or write sentences of your rules.

Name: _____

Date: _____

Directions: Cut out the cards. Then mix them up. Find the card that has the same meaning as the line or picture your teacher shows you.

I pledge allegiance to the flag of the United States of America

and to the Republic for which it stands

one Nation, under God, indivisible

with liberty and justice for all.

Songs for America
Grade One Lesson Plans

Objective

Understands how democratic values came to be, and how they have been exemplified by people, events, and symbols by knowing the Pledge of Allegiance and patriotic songs, poems, and sayings that were written long ago, and understands their significance. McREL K-4 History Standard 4, Level II-10

Materials

★ copies of *Patriotic Songs* (page 34)

★ copies of *Picturing the Songs* (page 35)

★ copies of *So Beautiful!* (page 36)

★ art supplies and blank paper

★ butcher paper

★ literature books *Yankee Doodle* illustrated by Patti Goodnow and *America the Beautiful* by Katharine Lee Bates (optional)

Procedure

1. If possible, have the music to "Yankee Doodle" or "America the Beautiful" playing as students walk into the room.

2. Place the words to the song "Yankee Doodle" on the board. You can find the words to this and "America the Beautiful" on *Patriotic Songs* (page 34). Allow students to sing the song aloud after you go over the words with them. Do the same for "America the Beautiful."

3. Explain to students that the songs are about the United States and fighting to keep it free, and about how wonderful it is. Ask them if the writers of the Constitution would agree with these songs. How would they feel about these songs?

4. Share the information from *Patriotic Songs* with the students. Ask the students if the meaning of the songs' lyrics is different from what they had imagined. You may choose to go over the definitions of the underlined words before reading it aloud to the students.

5. If there is time, read the books *Yankee Doodle* and *America the Beautiful* with the students. This will give them the opportunity to see pictures that go with the words of the songs.

6. After students have learned about the meaning of the songs, complete *Picturing the Songs* (page 35) as a class or individually.

7. Once students have completed their organizers, show them *So Beautiful!* (page 36) of the mountains in Colorado. This image can be found on the Library of Congress website at this URL address: http://hdl.loc.gov/loc.pnp/cph.3b49685. Ask the class if seeing the mountains would make them want to write a poem, as it did the author of "America the Beautiful." In pairs, have students complete the activity on *So Beautiful!*

8. To assess your students' learning, go over each activity in the *Bloom's Taxonomy Chart* (page 33) with the class. Assign each student an activity or allow them to choose their own. All of these activities are based on Bloom's Taxonomy of Cognitive Development.

9. Finally, for an extension, refer to the *Extension Activity* (page 33).

Songs for America
Grade One Lesson Plans *(cont.)*

Bloom's Taxonomy Chart

Knowledge: In the song "Yankee Doodle," what is a "macaroni?" Draw a picture to show the meaning.

Comprehension: Choose one line from "America the Beautiful." Paint a picture to show its meaning.

Application: Is there anything in the United States that makes you think of beauty? Find a picture in a magazine of something in nature that you find beautiful. Cut it out and glue it on to a piece of paper. Underneath, write one sentence that tells why that picture is beautiful.

Analysis: Use a T-chart to compare "Yankee Doodle" and "America the Beautiful."

Synthesis: With a partner, write a new patriotic song.

Evaluation: Which song is better, "Yankee Doodle" or "America the Beautiful?" Write a sentence telling which song you prefer and why you like it best.

Extension Activity

1 Divide the class into four groups. Give each group one of the following assignments.

★ Create a mural for the song "God Bless America" by Irving Berlin. Use paints, markers, or crayons to show what this song means.

★ Create posters to show what each line in "God Bless America" means. Cut pictures out of magazines or draw them on the poster.

★ Create actions for the song "Yankee Doodle." Show the meaning of the song through the actions.

★ Create instruments that can be played while singing "Yankee Doodle." You may choose to make a paper plate tambourine with bells, a drum out of old cans, or other homemade instruments. (This activity might be best for ELL or struggling students, as they do not have to show the meaning of the songs through their activity.)

2 Have each group show off their creations.

3 As a class, discuss how these assignments helped them better understand the meaning of the songs.

Name: _____

Date: _____

"Yankee Doodle" and "America the Beautiful" are called patriotic songs. When you are patriotic, you have a love for your country. These songs were written by people who loved their country.

"Yankee Doodle" is a very old song and started out in <u>Europe</u> many years ago. Then, the <u>British</u> sung it to tease the <u>colonists</u> during our war for freedom, the <u>Revolutionary War</u>. The colonists liked the song, so they sung it as they marched into battle. The word "macaroni" in the song is not a noodle we eat with cheese. It is a fancy, dressed-up person. The British soldiers said that just because the colonists stuck a feather in their hats, it wouldn't make them fancy, or a "macaroni."

> Yankee Doodle went to town
> A-riding on a pony
> Stuck a feather in his hat
> And called it macaroni.
> Yankee Doodle, keep it up
> Yankee Doodle dandy
> Mind the music and the step
> And with the girls be handy.

"America the Beautiful" was written by Katharine Lee Bates in 1893. She had just climbed a mountain called Pikes Peak in the state of Colorado. She wrote the poem, "America the Beautiful" after seeing the beautiful top of the mountain. Then, the poem was put to music. The song is very long, so only the first part is sung most of the time.

> "America the Beautiful"
> O beautiful for spacious skies,
> For amber waves of grain,
> For purple mountain majesties
> Above the fruited plain!
> America! America!
> God shed his grace on thee
> And crown thy good with brotherhood
> From sea to shining sea!

What pictures do you get in your mind as you hear the words to "America the Beautiful" or "Yankee Doodle?"

Directions: Choose one of the songs and draw a picture in the border below of what you think about when you hear that song.

Name: _____

Date: _____

Directions: With your partner, write a poem about these mountains. When you have finished, share your poem with the class.

Courtesy of The Library of Congress

_____

_____

_____

_____

_____

_____

_____

_____

Two Famous Americans
Grade Two Lesson Plans

Objective

Understands how democratic values came to be, and how they have been exemplified by people, events, and symbols, such as knowing the English colonists who became revolutionary leaders and fought for independence from England (e.g., George Washington and Ben Franklin.)
McREL K-4 History Standard 4, Level 1.1

Materials

★ copies of *Meeting Two Great Men Reader's Theater* (pages 40–41)

★ copies of *Who Am I?* (page 42)

★ copies of *Franklin and the Constitution* (page 43)

★ art supplies and blank paper

★ small brown paper bags

Procedure

1. Ask students if they have ever heard of Benjamin Franklin. What do they know about him? Have they ever heard of George Washington? What do they know about him? List their answers on the board.

2. Explain to students that they are going to be doing a reader's theater about the two men. Read *Meeting Two Great Men Reader's Theater* (pages 40–41) as a class. Since reader's theater concentrates on fluency and the understanding of the text, it is not necessary to use props or costumes. If you do not feel your students can read the skit fluently, you may also record the script as students follow along, using different voices for each character. Even though there are only six parts, allow the other members of the class to follow along as they read. Explain that the script can be read a couple more times so that everyone has a turn reading. The repeated readings will also help students with their fluency.

3. Before reading the script, go over the following words with the students: Continental Congress, colonies, Constitution, Declaration of Independence, England, and government.

4. After you have performed the reader's theater, pass out *Who Am I?* (page 42). Explain to students that you are going to read some facts about Benjamin Franklin and George Washington (*Franklin and Washington Facts*, page 38). Based on what they learned, they should write down or a draw a picture of that fact in the correct face on *Who Am I?* You may choose to do this activity as a class using a transparency of the organizer. If writing is too difficult for your students, there is a suggested symbol they can draw rather than writing.

5. After students have completed their organizers, show them *Franklin and the Constitution* (page 43). This image can be found on the Library of Congress website at this URL address: http://hdl.loc.gov/loc.pnp/cph.3d01737. As a class, complete *Franklin and the Constitution Questions and Activity* (page 38).

6. To assess your students' learning, go over each activity in the *Bloom's Taxonomy Chart* (page 39) with the class. Assign each student an activity or allow them to choose their own. All of these activities are based on Bloom's Taxonomy of Cognitive Development.

7. Finally, for an extension, refer to *Extension Activity* (page 39).

Two Famous Americans
Grade Two Lesson Plans (cont.)

Franklin and Washington Facts

★ I fought in the Revolutionary War. Who am I? (George Washington) Symbol = cannon

★ I became the first president of the United States. Who am I? (George Washington) Symbol = large number "1"

★ I invented bifocals. Who am I? (Ben Franklin) Symbol = glasses

★ I did not fight in the war, but I did sign the Declaration of Independence. Who am I? (Ben Franklin) Symbol = feather pen

★ I watched over the writing of the Constitution. I wanted the United States to be strong. Who am I? (George Washington) Symbol = eyes looking over the Constitution

Franklin and the Constitution Questions and Activity

1 Tell the students that this is a picture of Benjamin Franklin. He is speaking at the Constitutional Convention where people from each colony gathered to write the Constitution.

2 Ask students the following questions.

★ Who is in the picture?

★ What do you think they are doing?

★ What do you think Benjamin Franklin is saying to the other men who are there to write the new laws and freedoms in the Constitution?

3 Next, ask students to pretend they are Benjamin Franklin. Have them create a simple puppet using a brown paper bag and pieces of scrap paper.

4 Then, ask the students to think of a law they would like to have included in the Constitution. Go around the room, and let every student use their puppet to state the new laws that should be made.

5 Discuss the laws with the students and ask them if their laws go along with other things they have learned about our country, Benjamin Franklin, and the Constitution.

#10259—Celebrating Constitution Day

Two Famous Americans
Grade Two Lesson Plans *(cont.)*

Bloom's Taxonomy Chart

Knowledge: Make a list to show what you have learned about Benjamin Franklin and George Washington.

Comprehension: Choose either George Washington or Benjamin Franklin. Complete a painting to show everything you have learned about that person.

Application: Do you know anyone who has fought in a war like George Washington? Ask your family if they know someone who has fought in a war. Share what you learned with the class.

Analysis: Tell your teacher one way George Washington and Benjamin Franklin were alike and one way they were different. You may also create a Venn diagram for this activity.

Synthesis: Benjamin Franklin invented many things. He invented bifocals because he could not see well when he read. Create your own invention. Draw a picture of it and name it.

Evaluation: Do you think George Washington and Benjamin Franklin helped our country? Complete this sentence: George Washington and Benjamin Franklin helped our country by . . .

Extension Activity

Use *Meeting Two Great Men Reader's Theater* to complete the activity below.

1 Divide students into six groups and assign each group a character. Have the students in that group make a painting of that character.

Extension Activity *(cont.)*

2 Tell students that you are going to read a line from the reader's theater. If their character said that line, they should hold up their poster.

3 Read the following lines from the reader's theater.

★ The year is 1787. Thirty-nine men are gathered in a small room in Philadelphia, a city in Pennsylvania. They are going to write the Constitution. (*Mrs. Tution*)

★ No. But oh class! You are in for such a treat! The two men are George Washington and Benjamin Franklin! (*Mrs. Consty*)

★ I have worked on a newspaper and I like to invent things. I am working on something that will help me see better as I read. I think I will call them bifocals. (*Benjamin Franklin*)

★ Oh, I think my grandpa uses those when he reads! (*Eddie*)

★ I want the United States to have a strong government. So, it is my job to look over, or preside over the writing of the Constitution. (*Washington*)

★ Mr. Franklin, are you helping to write the Constitution, too? (*Lilly*)

4 Ask students what they think Lilly and Eddie learned on their field trip. Ask them if they would want to travel in a time machine to meet George Washington and Benjamin Franklin. If they did, what questions would they ask them?

Characters

Mrs. Consty, Mrs. Tution (teachers), Eddie Eagle, Lilly Liberty (students), Benjamin Franklin, George Washington

In a classroom, two teachers, Mrs. Consty and Mrs. Tution, have made a time machine. The students are about to take a field trip to the 1700s, where they will meet two amazing men that helped form the Constitution.

Mrs. Tution: Class, we have great news! Our time machine works!

Mrs. Consty: So, today we are going to go back in time. Are you ready?

Eddie: Where will we go first?

Lilly: I hope we get to meet someone famous!

Eddie: Oh, me too!

The class and the two teachers hop into the time machine.

Mrs. Tution: Our first stop will be a very special place.

Mrs. Consty: Yes, it is the place where the United States Constitution was written.

Mrs. Tution: The year is 1787. Thirty-nine men are gathered in a small room in Philadelphia, a city in Pennsylvania. They are going to write the Constitution. But, two very special men are expecting us.

Eddie: Who? Who?

Sally: Oh, let me guess! Is it the president?

Mrs. Consty: No, in 1787 we didn't have a president yet. But oh, class! You are in for such a treat! The two men are George Washington and Benjamin Franklin!

Lilly: Who are they?

Mrs. Tution: You are about to find out!

Franklin: Hello, class! We have been waiting for you.

Washington: Yes, and we can't wait to tell you all about ourselves.

Mrs. Consty: We are very eager to hear about you, too!

Eddie: Can George Washington start first? He was the first president of the United States.

Washington: Is that so? I have heard some talk about that, but I haven't become president yet.

Franklin: No, we are just now writing the Constitution. It will tell all of the people what laws and rights, or freedoms, we will have.

Lilly: Mr. Franklin, are you helping to write the Constitution, too?

Franklin: Why yes, I am. But, I do a lot of other things as well. I have worked on a newspaper, and I like to invent things. I am working on something that will help me see better as I read. I think I will call them bifocals.

Lilly: Bi-what?

Franklin: Bifocals. They make the words look bigger on a page. But, they will only be at the bottom of my glasses, so I can still see when I am not reading.

Eddie: Oh, I think my grandpa uses those when he reads!

Mrs. Tution: Mr. Franklin, would you mind telling the class about how you helped us get our freedom?

Franklin: Well, I didn't fight in the war like Mr. Washington did. He was a great general. But, I did sign the Declaration of Independence. This was a paper we sent to England. England was ruling the colonies at the time, and we wanted to be free from them. The Declaration of Independence told the King of England that we wanted to be free and we wanted our own rules.

Mrs. Consty: Mr. Washington, you helped fight for our freedom?

Washington: Yes, I was a general in the war for our freedom. We like to call that war the Revolutionary War. But, I like what we are doing now much better.

Eddie: You mean, writing the Constitution?

Washington: Yes, these laws are very important. I want the United States to have a strong government. So, it is my job to look over, or preside, during the writing of the Constitution.

Franklin: Mr. Washington, I don't mean to interrupt, but it is time to sign the Constitution.

Washington: Well, children, we must go now. Thank you for visiting us! I hope this Constitution will be a part of your life 200 years from now.

Mrs. Tution: Oh, Mr. Washington, we still follow the Constitution. We would like to thank you and Mr. Franklin for all the work you have done to make sure we are still free today.

Who Am I?
Student Reproducible

Name: _____

Date: _____

Directions: Your teacher will read a sentence that either Ben Franklin or George Washington would have said. If Franklin said it, write the sentence down in Franklin's outline. If Washington said it, write the sentence down in the outline of Washington.

Benjamin Franklin

George Washington

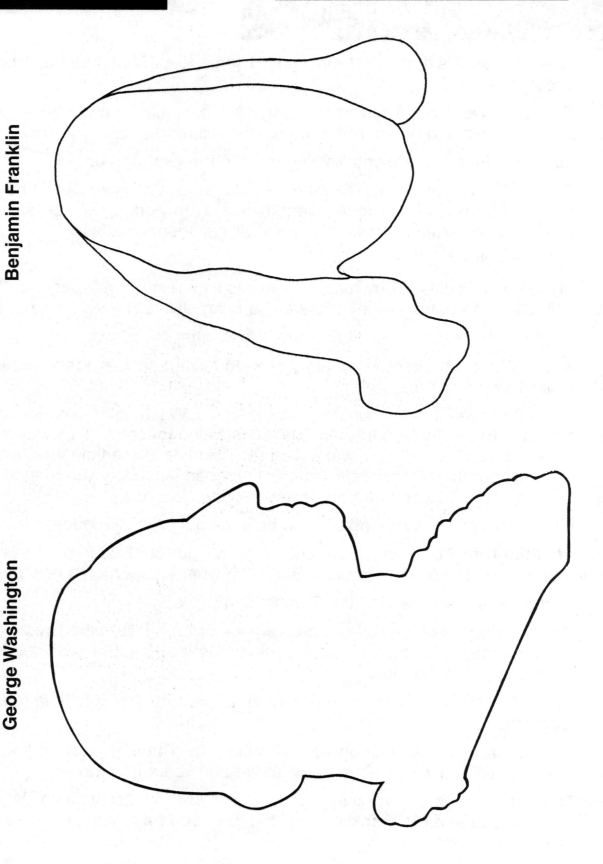

 #10259—Celebrating Constitution Day

Name: _____

Date: _____

Courtesy of The Library of Congress

Living in a Democracy
Grade Two Lesson Plans

Objective

Understands how democratic values came to be, and how they have been exemplified by people, events, and symbols by understanding ways in which such fundamental values as fairness, protection of individual rights, and responsibility for the common good have been applied by different groups of people (e.g., students and personnel in the local school.) McREL K-4 History Standard 4, Level 1.3

Materials

★ copies of *Living in a Democracy* (page 46)

★ copies of *Election* (page 47)

★ art supplies and blank paper

★ Copy of *Duck for President* by Doreen Cronin

Procedure

1 On the board, write the names of two different sports that the students can play during free time. Have students vote on their favorite sport by raising their hands.

2 Ask students how the class just decided which sport to play. Explain to them that they voted and the majority of votes won.

3 Write the word "democracy" on the board. Ask the class if they know what this word means. Explain to them that they live in a democracy. This means that in the United States, the people are allowed to make choices. They can choose what job to have, what church to go to, and who they want as president, along with other freedoms. The Constitution was written with democracy in mind.

4 Ask students to close their eyes as you read the following story to them.

You have just woken in the morning, still tired from your long evening of working in the fields. Your muscles ache and your hands have blisters. You wanted to come home earlier to get more rest ready for school, but the government told your family that they must grow enough wheat to feed the entire village, and you had to help. You wish that Mr. Mean wasn't the leader of your country. He isn't very nice. He tells the people what to do, and he doesn't give them the right to choose. But, since you don't live in a democracy, you do not have many freedoms.

5 Ask the students how they would feel if they lived in the country described above. What freedoms would they miss?

6 Give each student a copy of *Living in a Democracy* (page 46). Read the directions aloud and then have students cut out and organize each statement.

7 After students have completed their organizers, show them *Election* (page 47). This image can be found on the Library of Congress website at this URL address: http://hdl.loc.gov/loc.pnp/cph.3c17793. Complete *Election Questions and Activity* (page 45).

8 To assess your students' learning, go over each activity in the *Bloom's Taxonomy Chart* (page 45) with the class. Assign each student an activity or allow them to choose their own. All of these activities are based on Bloom's Taxonomy of Cognitive Development.

9 Finally, for an extension, read the book *Duck for President* by Doreen Cronin to the students and refer to *Extension Activity* (page 45).

Election Questions and Activity

1 Ask students the following questions.

★ Do people appear to take voting seriously?

★ What else do you notice about the picture? (lines forming of people wanting to vote)

★ Why would they stand in line that long just to vote?

★ Would it be worth it?

2 Have students complete the activity on *Election* (page 47).

Bloom's Taxonomy Chart

Knowledge: What is a democracy? Write the definition on a piece of paper.

Comprehension: Why do people vote? Write a sentence to explain your answer.

Application: What are freedoms you have in a democracy? Create a freedom banner listing all of the freedoms you can think of on a large sheet of paper. Draw pictures to show those freedoms.

Analysis: Compare your classroom to the United States. What freedoms do you have in your classroom that you also have living in the United States? List them on one side of T-chart labeled "Freedoms in the Class and the United States." On the other side of the T-chart, list freedoms you do not have in your classroom. Label that side of the chart "Freedoms We Don't Have in the Classroom."

Synthesis: The United States flag is a symbol of freedom. Create another flag that shows what a democracy is for someone that does not know what that word means.

Evaluation: In your opinion, what is the most important freedom you have as a person, living in the United States? Name that freedom and explain why it is most important.

Extension Activity

1 After reading the story *Duck for President* ask students to compare Duck and the other animals to the young child working in the fields from the paragraph read aloud in the lesson introduction. Were they in similar situations? How did Duck feel? Did he have a right to demand change?

2 Divide the class into four groups. Write "Duck" on two small pieces of paper and "Farmer Brown" on the other two. Have each group choose one of the slips of paper without looking. Then, tell each group that they are in charge of either Farmer Brown's or Duck's election campaign. They need to create a poster that would say why their candidate is the best person (or animal) to run the farm.

3 Next, allow them to convince the class with their posters.

4 Have the class vote for either Duck or Farmer Brown for farm leader.

5 After the votes are counted, ask the class if Duck lived in a democracy on the farm before the voting. Ask them why they like living in a democracy.

Name: _____

Date: _____

Directions: Cut out and read the sentences below. Organize the sentences in two piles. If the sentence would be said in a democracy, put it in a democracy pile. If it would be said in a country that is not a democracy, put the sentence in a second pile. When you have finished sorting them, glue the two piles onto a piece of paper and label them.

Every Sunday I go to the church my family chooses.

My mom and dad voted for president this year.

We must be home by 5:00 every night. Our ruler will not allow us out after that.

I want to go to college, but the government says I must work in the factory.

I get to choose what I want to be when I grow older.

The government said we cannot go to church anymore.

Name: _____

Date: _____

This photograph shows people voting.

Directions: Make a poster that shows another freedom we have because we live in a democracy. On your poster, show expressions on people's faces to show how they feel about that freedom and living in a democratic nation.

Courtesy of The Library of Congress

How Do We Make Laws?
Grade Two Lesson Plans

Objective

Understands the sources, purposes, and functions of law, and the importance of the rule of law for the protection of individual rights and the common good, as well as knowing that a good rule or law solves a specific problem, is fair, and does not go too far.
McREL Civics Standard 3, Level 1.6

Materials

★ copies of *How a Law Is Made* (page 50)

★ copies of *A Bill Becomes Law* (page 51)

★ copies of *Crazy Laws* (page 52)

★ art supplies and blank paper

Procedure

1. Prepare a sign to hang on the board that says, "New Rule: There are no rules this morning." As students come to class, allow them to act as if there are no rules in the classroom for about two minutes. Then, bring them together as a class.

2. Ask them how it felt to have no rules. What would happen if there were no rules for the rest of the day? What bad things might happen?

3. Explain to students that even though the United States is a democracy, we still must have laws. Laws protect the citizens and keep them safe. But how are laws made?

4. Tell students that there is a process that the United States Government has to go through before a law can be made. This process is written in the Constitution.

5. Split the class into two groups. The first group is the House of Representatives. The second group is the Senate. Choose one student to be president. You may want to draw a student's name from a jar to make the presidential choice easier. Create cardboard signs for each group and for the president to wear.

6. Explain to students that the House and the Senate make up Congress. That is part of our government. The United States Constitution says how a bill should become a law. It gives Congress and the president the right to create laws.

7. Show students *How a Law Is Made* (page 50) and explain each step to them.

8. Tell students that they are going to pass a law for the classroom. Give them three ideas for new laws, or create your own bill to propose. Let the House members decide which bill to pass on to the Senate. Have them vote on the bill, as well as change it, if they feel it is necessary. Complete the entire process of a bill becoming a law with the class. Some proposed bills might be: an extra three minutes at recess, Fridays shall be designated as bring an extra snack to school day, or once a month the class can have a pet show-and-tell.

9. After students have completed the process of a bill becoming a law, ask them to complete the activity on *How a Law is Made*.

10. Show students *A Bill Becomes Law* (page 51). This image can be found on the Library of Congress website at this URL address: http://hdl.loc.gov/loc.pnp/cph.3c11372. Complete *A Bill Becomes a Law Questions and Activity* (page 49).

Procedure *(cont.)*

11 To assess your students learning, go over each activity in the *Bloom's Taxonomy Chart* below with the class. Assign each student an activity or allow them to choose their own. All of these activities are based on Bloom's Taxonomy of Cognitive Development.

12 Finally, for an extension, refer to *Extension Activity* below.

A Bill Becomes a Law Questions and Activity

1 Ask students who they think is with the president as he is signing the bill. Do they think he asks other people for their opinions before passing a bill into a law?

2 Tell students that the bill he was signing in the picture was for veterans, or people who have fought in wars.

3 Put the students in pairs. With their partner, have them complete the activity on *A Bill Becomes Law* (page 51).

Bloom's Taxonomy Chart

Knowledge: What two choices does the president have when he sees a bill?

Comprehension: Write down how a bill becomes a law in three main steps using your own words.

Application: What are some rules you have in your classroom? What are some rules you have at home? Make a list of these rules.

Analysis: Why do you have rules in your classroom? Why do you have rules at home? Why do we have laws? Write a speech for your class, explaining why laws and rules are needed.

Synthesis: If you could pass a United States law, what would it be? Create a new bill you think should be made into a law.

Evaluation: Who has more power when signing a bill into law, the president, the House of Representatives, or the Senate? Why do you think that person or group has more power?

Extension Activity

1 Tell students that most laws in the United States are necessary for our safety and to help the country run smoothly. But some crazy laws have been passed, too.

2 Read the list of *Crazy Laws* (page 52) to the students. Then do the following activity.

3 Divide the students into six groups. Assign each group a law. Tell them to pretend that they are the people that created the law.

4 Have each group create a poster illustrating the law and answering the following questions: Why would they make such a law? What should happen if the law is broken?

5 Allow students time to share their posters with the class.

Name: _____

Date: _____

Directions: Label the pictures below to show how a bill becomes a law.

_____
_____
_____

_____
_____

_____
_____
_____

_____
_____
_____
_____

Name: _____

Date: _____

President Calvin Coolidge is signing a bill for veterans, or people who have fought in wars.

Courtesy of The Library of Congress

Directions: Make a list of what you think the bill might say.

_____

_____

_____

_____

_____

_____

_____

_____

_____

_____

_____

Crazy Laws
Student Reproducible

Name: _____

Date: _____

Directions: Choose one of the laws below. Pretend you are one of the people who came up with that law. Design a poster to illustrate the law. On the poster include the reason this law is needed and what will happen to anyone who breaks this law.

It's against the law to sing off key in North Carolina.

You may not ride a bicycle without having both your hands on the handlebars in a city in North Carolina.

Persons may be placed in jail for up to five years for shooting a hole in a penny anywhere in the United States.

It is against the law to throw a ball at someone's head for fun in New York.

Women may not drive in a housecoat in California.

Ice cream may not be eaten while standing on the side-walk in some towns in California.

A New Government
Grade Three Lesson Plans

Objective

Understands the accomplishments of ordinary people in historical situations and how each struggles for individual rights or for the common good.
McREL/Level 2/Standard 4/Number 4

Materials

★ copies of *A New Government* (page 56)

★ copies of *Voting for the Constitution* (page 57)

Procedure

1. Tell students there were many ideas of how the United States Government should be organized and it wasn't easy to get the thirteen states to agree on the laws of the Constitution. People disagreed on how much power the government should have and how much power should stay with the states. Ask students if they can imagine what it would be like if every state had its own money and its own president.

2. Split students into 13 groups, representing the 13 states of the early nation (some students may work individually, most will be in pairs).

3. Distribute *A New Government* (page 56) to each group and assign groups one of the following state names: Virginia, Delaware, Maryland, North Carolina, South Carolina, Georgia, New Hampshire, Massachusetts, Connecticut, New York, New Jersey, Pennsylvania, Rhode Island.

4. Allow students ample time to complete *A New Government*.

5. Have each of the 13 groups briefly present the government they created to the class.

6. Write the names of the 13 states on the board and vote by a show of hands on which government students think would be best for the nation, they may not vote for their own government. (Each state gets one vote for a total of 13 votes, so small groups will have to agree amongst themselves before casting their vote.)

7. Let students know that, just like in the history of the United States, they need a minimum of nine votes to ratify the Constitution.

8. Vote until one of the state's governments gets the required nine votes. If your class reaches an impasse, you might encourage them to compromise by offering a small reward if they can ratify the constitution within a given time.

9. Once one of the state's governments has received the necessary nine votes, discuss with the students the difficulty of reaching an agreement (or if they were unable to ratify one of the constitutions, discuss what made it impossible). Ask groups who didn't vote for the winning government how they feel. Do they think this constitution is fair? Would these groups choose to follow the laws, or would they decide to split off and form their own government? Tell students that the United States Constitution was ratified unanimously by all 13 states. What do students think is the importance of this unanimous decision? Are students surprised that 13 states were all able to agree on the same things?

A New Government
Grade Three Lesson Plans (cont.)

Procedure (cont.)

10 After students have completed their sheets, show them *Voting for the Constitution* (page 57) of the 13 states' voting record on the United States Constitution. This image can be found on the Library of Congress, American Memory website at this URL address: http://memory.loc.gov/ammem/ by typing in the key words "State Votes, 1788." Complete *Voting on the Constitution Questions* below with the students.

11 To assess your students' learning, go over each activity in the *Bloom's Taxonomy Chart* below with the class. Assign each student an activity or allow them to choose their own. All of these activities are based on Bloom's Taxonomy of Cognitive Development.

12 Finally, for an extension, refer to *Extension Activity* (page 55).

Voting on the Constitution Questions

Ask the students the following questions.

★ What do you think this document is?

★ What do the letters and numbers stand for?

★ Why are two columns empty?

★ What should have gone in those spaces?

★ Why was it necessary to have this document?

Bloom's Taxonomy Chart

Knowledge: List five of the first 13 states. Define the word "ratify" and write an explanation of what was needed to ratify the Constitution.

Comprehension: Why was it difficult to ratify the Constitution? Write a short description of the difficulties your class faced in trying to agree on one form of government.

Application: What strategies did states use to ratify the Constitution? Write a short description of how you were finally able to come to an agreement. Were you forced to compromise?

Analysis: How was this activity similar to what you imagine states went through? How was it different? Draw a T-chart and give it the title "Ratifying the Constitution in the United States and in the Classroom." Label one side of the chart "similarities" and the other side "differences." List at least three things you think this activity had in common with the real process and at least three ways you think this activity was different from the real process of ratifying the Constitution.

Synthesis: You voted on one form of government. Do you think it is the absolute best possible form? List three things you would add to your class constitution to make it better. The authors of the Constitution also added rules, called amendments, to the Constitution.

Evaluation: In your opinion, why was it important for most of the states to agree on the Constitution? Why was it important to have all of the states agree on the Constitution?

Extension Activity

1 Tell students that many people were involved in creating the Constitution and getting it ratified.

2 Ask students if they can name any of the men involved. Ask for suggestions as to why no women were involved.

3 List students' suggestions on the board and add any important names that are not mentioned. Be sure to include Alexander Hamilton, James Madison, John Jay, George Washington, Benjamin Franklin, Edmund Randolph and Roger Sherman.

4 Have students choose one name from the list and research that person to find out at least three interesting facts about them.

5 Students can present what they find in the form of a short bibliography with pictures or as a cartoon strip.

Directions: Use this sheet to make a government. Get ready to present your answers to the class.

1. How will you decide who is the next leader (will you vote or will there be another type of competition)?

   _____

   _____

2. Apart from the leader, what other groups will be in your government? What power will they have?

   _____

   _____

   _____

   _____

3. What power do regular people have in your government?

   _____

   _____

   _____

   _____

4. Write two laws for your government.

   _____

   _____

5. List at least two things that are special about your government.

   _____

   _____

   _____

   _____

Name: _____

Date: _____

Affirmative.   *Negative.*

Arti-cles.											
I.	N.H.	R.I.	Cy.N.J.P.		M.V.	N.C. S.C.		N.Y.	R.I. absent	N.J. N.J. P. absent absent	Dl. absent
II.	N.H.	R.I.		Cy.N.J.P.	D.M.V.	N.C. S.C.					
III.	N.H.	R.I.	Cy.N.J.P.	D.M.V.		N.C. S.C.					
IV.	N.H.	R.I.	Cy.N.J.P.	D.M.V.		N.C. S.C.					
V.	N.H.	R.I.	Cy.N.J.P.	D.M.V.		N.C. S.C.					
VI.	N.H.	R.I.	Cy.N.J.P.	D.M.V.		N.C. S.C.					
VII.	N.H.	R.I.	Cy.N.J.P.	D.M.V.		N.C. S.C.					
VIII.	N.H.	R.I.	Cy.N.J.P.	D.M.V.		N.C. S.C.					
IX.	N.H.	R.I.	Cy.N.J.P.	D.M.V.		N.C. S.C.					
X.	N.H.	R.I.	Cy.N.J.P.	D.M.V.		N.C. S.C.					
XI.	N.H.	R.I.	Cy.N.J.P.	D.M.V.		N.C. S.C.					
XII.	N.H.	R.I.	Cy.N.J.P.	D.M.V.		N.C. S.C.					

Courtesy of The Library of Congress

Checks and Balances
Grade Three Lesson Plans

Objective

Understands the basic ideas set forth in the U.S. Constitution.
McREL/Level 2/Standard 4/Number 1

Materials

★ copies of *Law Markers* (page 61) one for each group of four students

★ copies of *Fair and Unfair Slips* (page 62), one citizen slip for every student, then one executive branch slip, one legislative branch slip, and one judicial branch slip for each group

★ *The United States Constitution Excerpts* (page 63), copied onto an overhead

★ Overhead projector

★ two trays, one marked "Fair" and the other marked "Unfair" placed in a central area of your room

Procedure

1 In this lesson, students will represent the branches of the United States government. They will have to determine whether laws are fair or unfair. The game is played in multiple rounds, adding a branch of government each time. In the first few rounds, it will be hard to pass many fair laws, but as branches of government are added, students will be more successful. Read these rules of the first round of the game to your students:

★ You will be working with your classmates to determine the fairness of laws. I will distribute some law markers to the group. Some laws are fair and some are unfair. If you get a fair law, pass it to the next person in the circle. If you get an unfair law, take it to the "Unfair Tray." When a fair law goes around the entire circle, the last person may take it to the "Fair Tray."

★ Each of you will receive a slip of paper that tells you what some of the symbols on the law markers mean. When you get a law marker passed to you, use your slip of paper to decide whether to pass it on (if it's fair) or put it in the unfair tray (if it's unfair). If the symbol is not on your slip of paper, you have to guess whether it is a fair law or an unfair law.

★ Our goal is to see how many fair laws you can pass in three minutes, so do your best to move quickly.

★ Remember: Pass the fair laws and put the unfair ones in the tray. You may have to guess about which way the law should go.

2 Split students into groups of four and choose one group to demonstrate the game. Give each student in the demonstration group the "Citizen" slip from *Fair and Unfair Slips* (page 62). Give the first person in the circle a pile of *Law Markers* (page 61). Have the group demonstrate the game by passing around the law markers and sorting the fair and unfair laws. They will frequently have to guess whether a symbol means the law is fair or unfair. After they have passed a few markers around, stop the demonstration and answer any questions.

Procedure *(cont.)*

3 Prepare the other groups and start the game. When three minutes have passed, stop the game and tally the scores. To tally the scores take all the law markers out of the "Fair" tray and count the fair laws (square, circle, heart, and star) and subtract the unfair ones (without telling students which are which). Mark the scores for each group on the board. Discuss why it was difficult to pass fair laws.

4 For one student from each group, trade an "Executive Branch" slip (page 62) for his or her "Citizen" slip. Repeat the game and tally the scores. Discuss this round—what made the game easier?

5 For another student from each group, trade a "Legislative Branch" slip (page 62) for his or her "Citizen" slip. Repeat the game, tally scores, and discuss. Help students notice that sometimes when the citizens or the executive branch passes an unfair law, the legislative branch is able to stop it. By working together, these branches help ensure that no unfair laws are passed.

6 Finally, trade a "Judicial Branch" slip (page 62) for one student's "Citizen" slip in each group. Each member in a group should now have a different slip. Repeat the game, tally scores, and discuss.

7 Tell students that the authors of the United States Constitution organized the government so there would be "checks and balances," which means that it takes all three branches of government to create a law. This helps ensure that only fair laws are passed.

8 Show students *United States Constitution Excerpts* (page 63). An image of the Constitution can be found on the Our Documents website at this URL address: http://www.ourdocuments.gov/doc.php?flash=old&doc=9. Complete the *U.S. Constitution Excerpts Activity* below.

9 To assess your students learning, go over each activity in the *Bloom's Taxonomy Chart* (page 60) with the class. Assign each student an activity or allow them to choose their own. All of these activities are based on Bloom's Taxonomy of Cognitive Development.

10 Finally, for an extension, refer to the *Extension Activity* (page 60).

U.S. Constitution Excerpts Activity

1 Read aloud the excerpts from page 63. Have students follow along on their own copy if you wish.

2 Assist students in making the connection between the terms executive, judicial, and legislative to the common names they have likely heard (president, Supreme Court, Congress).

Checks and Balances
Grade Three Lesson Plans *(cont.)*

U.S. Constitution Excerpts Activity *(cont.)*

3 Help students understand that, just like in the game they played, these three branches of government use "checks and balances" to make sure only fair laws are passed. Read aloud and discuss the example of checks and balances.

4 Ask students whom they think holds the most power in the government. Help them see that by voting, citizens actually hold the most power.

Bloom's Taxonomy Chart

Knowledge: List the three branches of the United States Government and match the following terms with the appropriate branch: President, Supreme Court, House of Representatives, and Senate.

Comprehension: What is the system of "checks and balances?" Why is it important? Write and illustrate a short story describing what the United States might be like without this system.

Application: Checks and balances are like the game rock, paper, scissors, because each one stops one of the others. Work in a group of three to come up with another checks and balances game like rock, paper, scissors. Explain your game and teach the class how to play.

Analysis: How is the system of checks and balances different than the way your classroom works? Fold a piece of paper in half. Label one side "Classroom" and the other side "United States." On the classroom side, draw a picture of who has power and write why this arrangement is important. On the side labeled United States, draw a picture of who has power and write why this is important.

Bloom's Taxonomy Chart *(cont.)*

Synthesis: How do the citizens of the United States check and balance the government? Write a short description of how the people tell the government what to do.

Evaluation: Who do you think has the most power in the United States Government? On a piece of paper, draw a picture of the branch you think has the most power, and then underneath your drawing write a short explanation of your opinion.

Extension Activity

Mark some unfair laws "Fair to You" on each type of slip. For example, you could mark a square "Fair to You" on the Judicial Branch slip. Play the game and tally the fair-to-you laws that are passed, giving these points only to the branch that they benefit. These points represent power. Which branch ended up with the most power? Discuss checks and balances in terms of misuse of power and the passing of laws that benefit only certain groups.

Law Markers
Student Reproducible

Fair and Unfair Slips
Student Reproducible

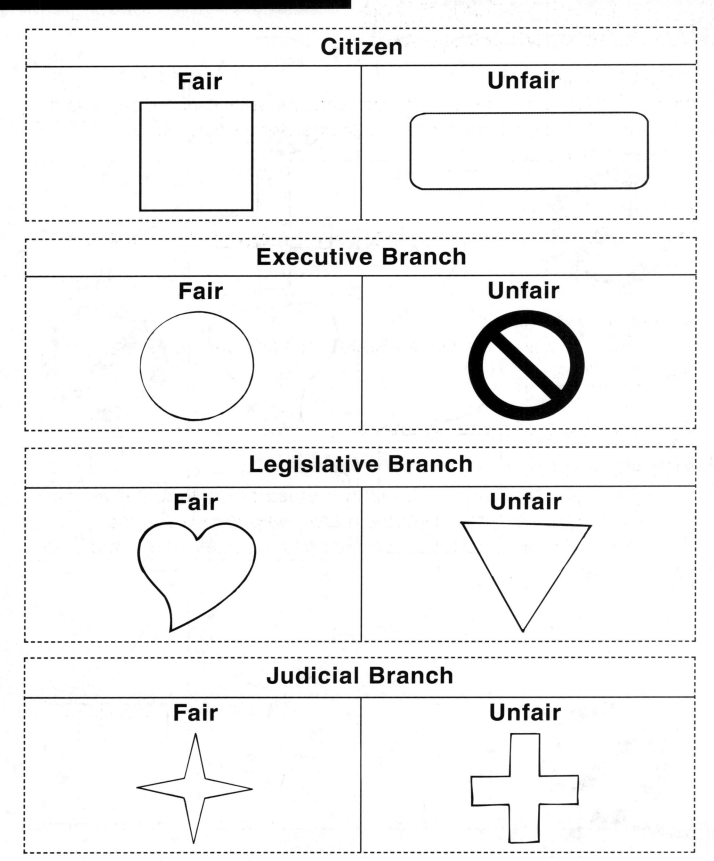

Citizen

Fair	Unfair

Executive Branch

Fair	Unfair

Legislative Branch

Fair	Unfair

Judicial Branch

Fair	Unfair

 #10259—*Celebrating Constitution Day*

Name: _____

Date: _____

Article I. Section 1.

All legislative Powers herein granted shall be vested in a Congress of the United States, which shall consist of a Senate and House of Representatives.

Article II. Section 1.

The executive Power shall be vested in a President of the United States of America.

Article III. Section 1.

The judicial Power of the United States, shall be vested in one Supreme Court . . .

Example of Checks and Balances:

Article I. Section 7.

Every Bill which shall have passed the House of Representatives and the Senate, shall, before it become a Law, be presented to the President of the United States; If he approve he shall sign it, but if not he shall return it . . .

The Bill of Rights
Grade Three Lesson Plans

Objective

Understands the basic principles of American democracy (e.g. right to life, liberty, pursuit of happiness, equality of opportunity, etc.)
McREL/Level 2/Standard 4/Number 2

Materials

★ copies of *Bill of Rights Illustrations* (pages 67–68)

★ copies of *Bill of Rights Document* (page 69)

Procedure

1 Tell your class that the Bill of Rights was an important addition to the Constitution. The Bill of Rights includes ten rules that help ensure the government doesn't have too much power over the rights of the people. These ten rules show what the people who founded the United States believed in.

2 Display and quickly preview the eight *Bill of Rights Illustrations* (pages 67–68). Tell students that these pictures represent eight of the 10 rules in the Bill of Rights. Students will be writing a short description of the idea they think is shown in each illustration and will then be trying to match the pictures to the real rule in the Bill of Rights.

3 Discuss the first illustration and ask students to write a short description of what they think is going on in the scene. Depending on your class, this description can be as short as a caption or a few words describing things or ideas they see (for example, religion or soldiers). Continue this procedure with the remaining illustrations, intentionally displaying them out of order.

4 On your classroom board, write the following short wordings of the first eight articles of the Bill of Rights (you could also do this before starting the lesson):

1. Freedom of religion

2. Right to bear arms

3. You don't have to house soldiers

4. The government can't search your house without a reason

5. You don't have to be a witness against yourself

6. Right to trial by jury

7. You can only be tried once for a crime

8. No cruel or unusual punishment

5 Review the eight illustrations using the following procedure:

★ Display an illustration

★ Ask volunteers to share what they wrote about the illustration

★ Try to match the illustration with one of the eight articles you listed on the board

★ Discuss why each right was/is important to people in the United States

Procedure *(cont.)*

6 After the discussion, show students *Bill of Rights Document* (page 69). This image can be found on the National Archives website at this URL address: http://www.ourdocuments.gov/doc.php?doc=13. Complete *Bill of Rights Questions and Activity* below.

7 To assess your students learning, go over each activity in the *Bloom's Taxonomy Chart* (page 66) with the class. Assign each student an activity or allow them to choose their own. All of these activities are based on Bloom's Taxonomy of Cognitive Development.

8 Finally, for an extension, refer to *Extension Activity* (page 66).

Bill of Rights Questions and Activity

1 Have students work in small groups to answer the following questions.

★ How many amendments were originally made to the Constitution?

★ How many amendments in total have been made to the Constitution?

★ What freedoms are specifically included in the Bill of Rights?

★ The First Amendment of the Bill of Rights includes the freedom of speech. Why is this freedom important.

★ A phrase used in courtrooms is "I plead the fifth." What right does the Fifth Amendment provide?

★ What amendments do you think are not needed today?

2 Bring the groups back together and discuss the answers as a class.

3 Ask students to research the constitution of your state. Have them find out if it provides rights for individual citizens? Students should create a chart comparing the rights listed in your state's constitution with the rights included in the Bill of Rights.

4 As a final activity, have students work in pairs to produce a bill of rights for the classroom.

Bloom's Taxonomy Chart

Knowledge: In your own words, list three of the amendments included in the Bill of Rights.

Comprehension: Why was the Bill of Rights important? Illustrate and describe in words what you think are the two most important freedoms guaranteed by the Bill of Rights.

Application: What are your rights? Work with a partner to write and illustrate at least four rights you have as a student and a person.

Analysis: Why do you think the Bill of Rights was needed? Imagine a situation that would make writing these amendments necessary. Draw a picture of this situation and then write the amendment that fixes it.

Synthesis: Working with a partner, pick your favorite amendment. Imagine one of you is for the amendment and the other is against it (even if you are both actually in favor of it). Argue why the amendment should or should not be kept as part of the Constitution.

Evaluation: The amendments included in the Bill of Rights were very important when they were written, but do any of these amendments seem strange today? Pick one of these amendments and write on a piece of paper why it should not be kept as part of the Constitution.

Extension Activity

1. Read aloud the last two amendments included in the Bill of Rights.

   Amendment IX

   The enumeration in the Constitution, of certain rights, shall not be construed to deny or disparage others retained by the people.

   Amendment X

   The powers not delegated to the United States by the Constitution, nor prohibited by it to the states, are reserved to the states respectively, or to the people.

2. Have students discuss these difficult amendments and try to create short descriptions like those listed in step four of this lesson.

3. Ask students to complete the set of descriptions by drawing the remaining two images.

Name: _____

Date: _____

Directions: Underneath each picture, write a short description explaining what you think is happening.

_____
_____

_____
_____

_____
_____

_____
_____

Name: _____

Date: _____

Directions: Underneath each picture, write a short description explaining what you think is happening.

_____

_____

_____

_____

_____

_____

_____

_____

Name: _____

Date: _____

Directions: Which words do you think are important in this document? Why do you think these are important? What do you notice about the layout of the document?

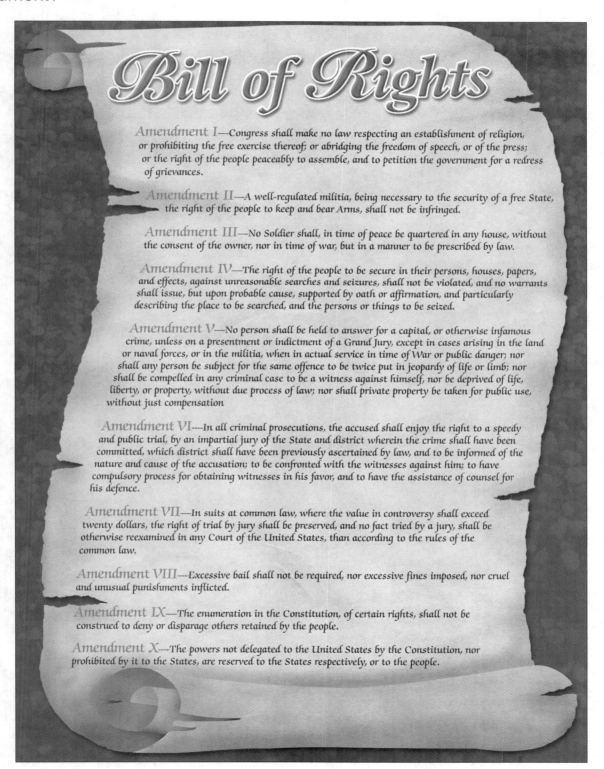

Bill of Rights

Amendment I—Congress shall make no law respecting an establishment of religion, or prohibiting the free exercise thereof; or abridging the freedom of speech, or of the press; or the right of the people peaceably to assemble, and to petition the government for a redress of grievances.

Amendment II—A well-regulated militia, being necessary to the security of a free State, the right of the people to keep and bear Arms, shall not be infringed.

Amendment III—No Soldier shall, in time of peace be quartered in any house, without the consent of the owner, nor in time of war, but in a manner to be prescribed by law.

Amendment IV—The right of the people to be secure in their persons, houses, papers, and effects, against unreasonable searches and seizures, shall not be violated, and no warrants shall issue, but upon probable cause, supported by oath or affirmation, and particularly describing the place to be searched, and the persons or things to be seized.

Amendment V—No person shall be held to answer for a capital, or otherwise infamous crime, unless on a presentment or indictment of a Grand Jury, except in cases arising in the land or naval forces, or in the militia, when in actual service in time of War or public danger; nor shall any person be subject for the same offence to be twice put in jeopardy of life or limb; nor shall be compelled in any criminal case to be a witness against himself, nor be deprived of life, liberty, or property, without due process of law; nor shall private property be taken for public use, without just compensation

Amendment VI—In all criminal prosecutions, the accused shall enjoy the right to a speedy and public trial, by an impartial jury of the State and district wherein the crime shall have been committed, which district shall have been previously ascertained by law, and to be informed of the nature and cause of the accusation; to be confronted with the witnesses against him; to have compulsory process for obtaining witnesses in his favor, and to have the assistance of counsel for his defence.

Amendment VII—In suits at common law, where the value in controversy shall exceed twenty dollars, the right of trial by jury shall be preserved, and no fact tried by a jury, shall be otherwise reexamined in any Court of the United States, than according to the rules of the common law.

Amendment VIII—Excessive bail shall not be required, nor excessive fines imposed, nor cruel and unusual punishments inflicted.

Amendment IX—The enumeration in the Constitution, of certain rights, shall not be construed to deny or disparage others retained by the people.

Amendment X—The powers not delegated to the United States by the Constitution, nor prohibited by it to the States, are reserved to the States respectively, or to the people.

Notes

Culminating Activity

Objective

Understands the basic ideas set forth in the United States Constitution, and the figures responsible for this document. McREL/Level 2/Standard 4

Materials

★ copies of *Famous American* (page 74)

★ copies of *Monument Plans* (page 75)

★ copies of *Connecting the Branches* (page 76)

★ art supplies

Procedure

1 Students will create exhibits for the Constitution Memorial Museum. Students at the various grade levels will contribute by creating an exhibit based on a famous American related to our Constitution. The connection can be direct, or indirect, but the student should understand the relationship.

2 Begin by re-examining the basic parts of the Constitution and reviewing previous activities. Students need to have at least a minimal understanding of the Constitution's core concepts in order to complete this activity. They should know about its beginnings and its core concept–three branches of government, no branch too powerful. Ask students the *United States Constitution Questions* (page 72).

3 Explain to the students that in order to understand and remember the Constitution, they will be creating a display about one person related to the document. Explain that they will get to choose from a list that you will provide.

4 Allow students to choose a famous American from the list below. Feel free to add to each category if you are inclined. At least one exhibit should be created from each category to add to the diversity of your museum.

★ John Jay, Alexander Hamilton, James Madison, George Washington, Benjamin Franklin (framers of the Constitution)

★ Strom Thurman, Hillary Clinton, Bill Frist, Edward Kennedy, local legislators (legislative branch)

★ Thomas Jefferson, Abraham Lincoln, Dwight D. Eisenhower, George W. Bush (executive branch)

★ John Jay, John Marshall, Earl Warren, Sandra Day O'Connor, Thurgood Marshall (judicial branch)

6 Once students have chosen the subject of their exhibit, they should fill out *Famous American* (page 74). Younger students (kindergarten and first grade) should not be expected to do this part. You might have to assist the students in finding information either at the school library, classroom library, or on the Internet. If it is too time-consuming to gather this much information, you may be more selective in what your students choose. Limit the names in each category and supply the research on the few that remain.

Culminating Activity
(cont.)

Procedure (cont.)

7 Next, have the students create a monument or memorial to their chosen person. Any type of media is acceptable—crayons, watercolor, oil pastels, markers, paint. Encourage creativity and do not make the choices too restrictive. Provide multiple ideas for their creations so that students can expand their perspective and not limit themselves to the typical illustration. They can use this opportunity to make dioramas, papier mache models, 3-D pictures, clay formations, etc. If they do choose to draw, persuade them to produce something out of the ordinary.

8 After all students have created their displays, assemble the pieces in a large classroom, library, or auditorium. Students may first share their items individually in their own classrooms.

9 To assess your students learning, go over each activity in the *Bloom's Taxonomy Chart* (page 73) with the class. Assign each student an activity or allow them to choose their own. All of these activities are based on Bloom's Taxonomy of Cognitive Development.

10 Finally, for an extension, refer to *Extension Activity* (page 73).

United States Constitution Questions

★ What are the first ten amendments of the Constitution known as, and what do they do?

★ What are the three branches of government and why is it important to have all three?

★ Where was the Constitutional Convention held?

★ Name two symbols in America that represent what the Constitution means to you. Explain how they represent the Constitution.

★ Why was the Constitution written?

★ What was the Declaration of Independence? From what country did we want to be free?

★ Name three people that signed the Constitution.

★ List and describe two amendments made to the Constitution.

★ Is the Constitution still important today? If so, how?

Culminating Activity
(cont.)

Bloom's Taxonomy Chart

Knowledge: Make a list of everything you learned about the Constitution.

Comprehension: Compare one right from the Bill of Rights to a right you have in your classroom. How are they similar? How are they different? Use a Venn diagram or a T-chart to compare them.

Application: How does the Constitution affect you and your family? Draw a picture to show how it has an impact on you or your family. Write a caption for the picture. For example, if your mother works for a newspaper, then the Bill of Rights affects her in that she has freedom of the press and freedom of speech.

Analysis: Place the following in order of importance by putting a 1, 2, 3, and 4 next to them, with one being the most important: The Declaration of Independence, the Bill of Rights, the 19th Amendment, and the 15th Amendment. Then, explain why you numbered them the way you did.

Synthesis: Create a Constitution for your family. What rights should you have within your family? What laws, or rules, should you have? Draw your original Constitution on a poster.

Evaluation: Which amendment from the Bill of Right is the most important, in your opinion? Write down which amendment is the most important, along with two reasons why you feel it is. Give your reasons to the class to see if they agree or disagree with you.

Extension Activity

1 Students should pretend they are curators of the Constitution Memorial Museum. They should each create a brochure that would highlight the exhibits found in the museum.

2 Their brochures should include a cover, with a picture of the museum on it; descriptions and pictures of three to five artifacts found in the museum, interesting facts about the Constitution, and a layout of the museum.

3 When they have finished their brochures, students may attempt to find relationships between their items and other items in the museum.

4 Using *Connecting the Branches* (page 76), students in groups of three or four can work together to categorize the various exhibits in the museum based on branch of government.

Famous American
Student Reproducible

Name: _____

Date: _____

Directions: Use this page to research your chosen American.

Name of the person: _____

Their date of birth: _____

Their place of birth: _____

Which branch does your American represent? (Circle one)

Legislative   Executive   Judicial   Other

If you circled "Other," explain.

_____

_____

What were your American's job responsibilities? List at least two and explain.
Why was this person important?

_____

_____

_____

In the space below, brainstorm about the American you have chosen.

Name: _____

Date: _____

Directions: In the space below, plan your monument or memorial. Be sure to include a name for it and labels to show what materials you plan to use.

Name: _____

Materials I will need: _____

_____

_____

Use the space below to draw a picture of your monument or memorial.

Name: _____

Date: _____

Directions: Look at all of the completed exhibits. Make three lists to show which exhibits are related to each branch.

Legislative: _____

_____

_____

Executive: _____

_____

_____

Judicial: _____

_____

_____

Which branch has the most exhibits? _____

_____

Why do you think that is?

_____

_____

_____

Which is your favorite exhibit? Write a sentence to describe what it is and why you like it.

_____

_____

_____

Standards Correlations

Lesson Title	McREL Content Standard
National Symbols	Understands how democratic values came to be, and how they have been exemplified by people, events, and symbols, such as knowing the history of American symbols. McREL K-4 History Standard 4, Level 1.8.
Being a Classroom Citizen	Understands how democratic values came to be, and how they have been exemplified by people, events, and symbols by understanding ways in which such fundamental values as fairness, protection of individual rights, and responsibility for the common good have been applied by different groups of people (e.g., students and personnel in the local school.) McREL K-4 History Standard 4, Level 1.3
Democracy in the Classroom	Understands how democratic values came to be, and how they have been exemplified by people, events, and symbols by understanding ways in which such fundamental values as fairness, protection of individual rights, and responsibility for the common good have been applied by different groups of people (e.g., students and personnel in the local school.) McREL K-4 History Standard 4, Level 1.3
What Does the Pledge Mean, Anyway?	Understands how democratic values came to be, and how they have been exemplified by people, events, and symbols by knowing the Pledge of Allegiance and patriotic songs, poems, and sayings that were written long ago, and understands their significance. McREL K-4 History Standard 4, Level II-10
Songs for America	Understands how democratic values came to be, and how they have been exemplified by people, events, and symbols by knowing the Pledge of Allegiance and patriotic songs, poems, and sayings that were written long ago, and understands their significance. McREL K-4 History Standard 4, Level II-10
Two Famous Americans	Understands how democratic values came to be, and how they have been exemplified by people, events, and symbols by understanding ways in which such fundamental values as fairness, protection of individual rights, and responsibility for the common good have been applied by different groups of people (e.g., students and personnel in the local school.) McREL K-4 History Standard 4, Level 1.1
Living in a Democracy	Understands how democratic values came to be, and how they have been exemplified by people, events, and symbols by understanding ways in which such fundamental values as fairness, protection of individual rights, and responsibility for the common good have been applied by different groups of people (e.g., students and personnel in the local school.) McREL K-4 History Standard 4, Level 1.3
How Do We Make Laws?	Understands the sources, purposes, and functions of law, and the importance of the rule of law for the protection of individual rights and the common good, as well as knowing that a good rule or law solves a specific problem, is fair, and does not go too far. McREL Civics Standard 3, Level 1.6
A New Government	Understands the accomplishments of ordinary people in historical situations and how each struggles for individual rights or for the common good. McREL/Level 2/Standard 4/Number 4
Checks and Balances	Understands the basic ideas set forth in the U.S. Constitution. McREL/Level 2/Standard 4/Number 1
The Bill of Rights	Understands the basic principles of American democracy (e.g. right to life, liberty, pursuit of happiness, equality of opportunity, etc.) McREL/Level 2/Standard 4/Number 2
Culminating Activity	Understands the basic ideas set forth in the United States Constitution, and the figures responsible for this document. McREL/Level 2/Standard 4

Resources

Resources List

★ **ABYZ News Links**—Newspapers and other news sources from around the world
http://www.abyznewslinks.com/

★ **America on the Move**—http://americanhistory.si.edu/onthemove/

★ **The American Presidency**—http://americanhistory.si.edu/presidency/

★ **American Rhetoric**—Famous speeches both as recordings and as written transcripts
http://www.americanrhetoric.com/

★ **The Avalon Project at Yale Law School**—History and political documents
http://www.yale.edu/lawweb/avalon/avalon.htm

★ **Colonial Williamsburg**—http://www.history.org/

★ **African American Experience**—http://www.history.org/Almanack/life/Af_Amer/aalife.cfm

★ **Colonial Williamsburg Multimedia Pages**—http://www.history.org/media/index.cfm

★ **Politics in Colonial America**—http://www.history.org/Almanack/life/politics/polhdr.cfm

★ **Eyewitness History.com**—Eyewitness accounts of historical events
http://www.eyewitnesstohistory.com/

★ **Hanover Historical Texts Project**—Primary sources dating from ancient to modern times.
http://history.hanover.edu/project.html

★ **History Place—Sounds of Presidents**—Presidential speeches and announcements
http://www.historyplace.com/specials/sounds-prez/

★ **Internet History Sourcebooks Project**—Public domain historical texts
http://www.fordham.edu/halsall/

★ **The Library of Congress**—http://www.loc.gov

   ★ American Memory—http://memory.loc.gov/ammem/

   ★ Global Gateway—http://international.loc.gov/intldl/intldlhome.html

   ★ America's Library—http://www.americaslibrary.gov

   ★ Thomas (legislative updates)—http://thomas.loc.gov/

   ★ Learning Page for Teachers—http://memory.loc.gov/learn1

   ★ American Folklife Center—http://www.loc.gov/folklife/

   ★ Veterans History Project—http://www.loc.gov/vets/

★ **The National Archives and Records Administration**—http://www.archives.gov/

   ★ Archival Research Catalog—http://www.archives.gov/research_room/arc/index.html

   ★ Digital Classroom—http://www.archives.gov/digital_classroom/index.html

   ★ History in the Raw—http://www.archives.gov/digital_classroom/history_in_the_raw.html

Resources List (cont.)

★ **The National Archives and Records Administration** (cont.)

  ★ Presidential Libraries and Museums—
  http://www.archives.gov/presidential_libraries/index.html

  ★ These libraries are located in presidential hometowns or birth sites:
  Herbert Hoover (Iowa)
  Franklin D. Roosevelt (New York)
  Harry S. Truman (Missouri)
  Dwight D. Eisenhower (Kansas)
  John F. Kennedy (Massachusetts)
  Lyndon B. Johnson (Texas)
  Gerald Ford (Michigan)
  James Carter (Arkansas)
  Ronald Reagan (California)
  George Bush (Texas)
  William Clinton (Arkansas)
  The Nixon Library (California) is privately operated by a foundation. The Nixon papers (currently housed in the National Archives) are in the process of being transferred to the Nixon Library. At that time the Nixon Library will become part of the National Archives.

★ **National History Day**—Main site for people interested in this yearly history competition
http://www.nationalhistoryday.org/

★ **New York Public Library**—Collections of digitized primary sources
http://www.nypl.org/digital/

★ **Our Documents**—100 milestone documents in American history
http://www.ourdocuments.gov/

★ **Political Cartoons and Cartoonists**—Digital copies of political cartoons throughout history
http://www.boondocksnet.com/gallery/pc_intro.html

★ **Smithsonian Institution**—http://www.si.edu/

★ **Teacher Created Materials**—Exploring History through Primary Sources kits and Primary Source Readers books
http://www.teachercreatedmaterials.com/socialstudies